W9-BGE-146

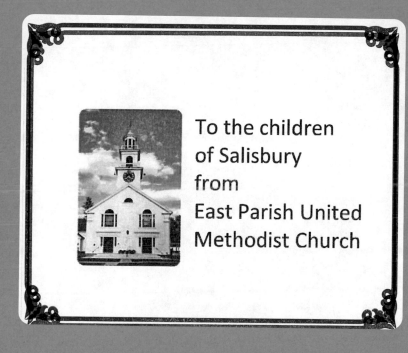

To the children
of Salisbury
from
East Parish United
Methodist Church

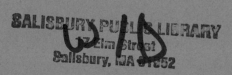
SALISBURY PUBLIC LIBRARY
Elm Street
Salisbury, MA 01952

National Park Explorers

DEATH VALLEY

by Sara Gilbert

CREATIVE EDUCATION · CREATIVE PAPERBACKS

TABLE OF CONTENTS

Death Valley is known for its low places.

WELCOME TO DEATH VALLEY NATIONAL PARK!

4

There is so much sand! The wind makes ripples in the **dunes**. People call this place Death Valley.

But this huge area in California and Nevada is not dead. It became a national park in 1994.

★ *Death Valley National Park*
■ *California* ■ *Nevada*

A beavertail cactus (above); a desert horned lizard (right)

DRY IN THE DESERT

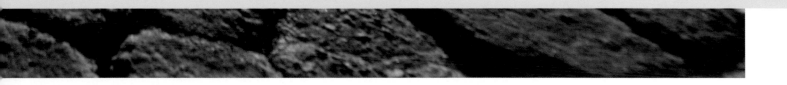

Death Valley is mostly **desert**. It is one of the hottest places on Earth. Only two inches (5.1 cm) of rain falls every year.

9

The earth is dry and cracked. Sand dunes stretch for miles. But there are also snow-covered mountains in the park.

Badwater Basin and Panamint Range (above); Mesquite Flat Dunes (right)

DESERT ADAPTATIONS

More than 1,000 kinds of plants grow here. Some have long roots to reach water deep underground. When it rains, wildflowers bloom.

13

Desert **tortoises** sleep underground. Bighorn sheep and other animals stay in the mountains. It is cooler there.

A desert bighorn (below); a desert tortoise (right)

BEAT THE HEAT

Almost one million people visit each year. Most of them come between October and April. The weather is not as hot then. They hike, watch birds, and camp.

The park is still open in the summer. You can talk to **rangers**. They will tell you stories about the sites.

Wildrose Charcoal Kilns (above); Harmony Borax Works (right)

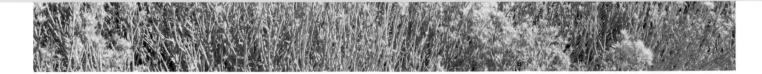

You can drive through the park in a car. Always take water and a map. You do not want to get lost in the desert!

Park visitors try to stay safe in the desert heat.

20

Activity

MINI DEATH VALLEY

Materials needed:
Empty shoebox
Colored paper
Scissors
Glue
Markers or crayons
Sand, sticks, and stones

Step 1: Set the shoebox on one side so that the opening faces you.

Step 2: Glue the colored paper to the inside walls of the shoebox. What colors would you see in Death Valley in summer? What about winter? Draw pictures on the paper, or glue cutout shapes.

Step 3: Put the sand, sticks, and stones in the box. You can glue them to the base, or just set them in the box. What else might you see in Death Valley? What animals would be there?

Step 4: Show your model Death Valley to a friend. Tell how it might be different at day or night, or in a different season.

Glossary

desert — a hot, dry land that gets little rain

dunes — piles of sand formed by the wind

rangers — people who take care of a park

tortoises — plant-eating, shelled animals that live on land

Read More

McHugh, Erin. *National Parks: A Kid's Guide to America's Parks, Monuments, and Landmarks.* New York: Black Dog & Leventhal, 2012.

National Geographic. *National Geographic Kids National Parks Guide U.S.A.: The Most Amazing Sights, Scenes, and Cool Activities from Coast to Coast.* Washington, D.C.: National Geographic Society, 2012.

Websites

Kids Discover: National Parks
http://www.kidsdiscover.com/spotlight/national-parks-for-kids/
See pictures from the parks and learn more about their history.

WebRangers
http://www.nps.gov/webrangers/
Visit the National Park Service's site for kids to find fun activities.

Note: Every effort has been made to ensure that the websites listed above are suitable for children, that they have educational value, and that they contain no inappropriate material. However, because of the nature of the Internet, it is impossible to guarantee that these sites will remain active indefinitely or that their contents will not be altered.

Index

Published by Creative Education and Creative Paperbacks
P.O. Box 227, Mankato, Minnesota 56002 • Creative Education
and Creative Paperbacks are imprints of The Creative Company
www.thecreativecompany.us

Design and production by Christine Vanderbeek
Art direction by Rita Marshall
Printed in the United States of America

Photographs by Alamy (Danita Delimont, Ariadne Van Zandbergen),
Corbis (Walter Bibikow/info@awl-images.com/JAI, Walter Bibikow/
JAI, Richard Cummins, Rolf Hicker/All Canada Photos, Jon Hicks,
Nick Saunders/All Canada Photos, Owen Smith), Dreamstime
(Wisconsinart), Getty Images (Kick Images), Shutterstock
(Tarchyshnik Andrei, Bufo, Don Fink, bogdan ionescu, Kelly-
Nelson, Jeffrey T. Kreulen, Yuri Kriventsoff, MNI, Dean Pennala,
Nelson Sirlin, Son Gallery, Nickolay Stanev, Tom Tietz, tobkatrina,
worldswildlifewonders)

Copyright © 2016 Creative Education, Creative Paperbacks
International copyright reserved in all countries. No part of this
book may be reproduced in any form without written permission
from the publisher.

Library of Congress Cataloging-in-Publication Data
Gilbert, Sara. • Death Valley / by Sara Gilbert. • p. cm. — (National
park explorers) • *Summary*: A young explorer's introduction to
California and Nevada's Death Valley National Park, covering
its desert landscape, plants, animals such as desert tortoises, and
activities such as bird-watching. • Includes index. • ISBN 978-1-
60818-630-3 (hardcover) • ISBN 978-1-62832-238-5 (pbk) • ISBN
978-1-56660-667-7 (eBook) • 1. Death Valley (Calif. and Nev.)—
Juvenile literature. I. Title.

F868.D2G55 2015
578.09794'87—dc23   2014048722

CCSS: RI.1.1, 2, 3, 4, 5, 6, 7, 10; RI.2.1, 2, 3, 5, 6, 7; RI.3.1, 3, 5, 7;
RF.1.1, 3, 4; RF.2.4

First Edition HC. 9 8 7 6 5 4 3 2 1
First Edition PBK 9 8 7 6 5 4 3 2 1